Bibliographical Series
of Supplements to 'British Book News'
on Writers and Their Work

★

GENERAL EDITOR
Bonamy Dobrée

¶ EDMUND BURKE was born in Dublin in January 1729. He died on 9 July 1797 and was buried at Beaconsfield.

EDMUND BURKE
from a wax medallion of 1791, by T. R. POOLE *in the*
National Portrait Gallery

EDMUND BURKE

by T. E. UTLEY

PUBLISHED FOR

THE BRITISH COUNCIL

and the NATIONAL BOOK LEAGUE

BY LONGMANS, GREEN & CO., LONDON, NEW YORK, TORONTO

LONGMANS, GREEN & CO. LTD.
6 & 7 Clifford Street, London W.1
Boston House, Strand Street, Cape Town
605–611 Lonsdale Street, Melbourne, C.1

LONGMANS, GREEN & CO. INC.
55 Fifth Avenue, New York 3

LONGMANS, GREEN & CO.
20 Cranfield Road, Toronto 16

ORIENT LONGMANS PRIVATE LTD.
Calcutta Bombay Madras
Delhi Hyderabad Dacca

First published in 1957

Printed in Great Britain at The Curwen Press, Plaistow, E.13

EDMUND BURKE

I

THE influence of Edmund Burke on the theory and
practice of British politics during the last hundred and
fifty years has been unique. No even approximate
parallel to it can be found. It is impossible, for example, to
think of any British statesman of whom it might be truth-
fully said that his mind had been formed by Locke or Hobbes,
yet it is equally impossible to think of any outstanding
English parliamentarian during this period of whom it can
be said that he altogether escaped the influence of Burke.
Nevertheless, Burke was not merely a teacher of the tech-
niques of political life; he was no mere Machiavelli of parliamentary government, taking its ends and origins for granted
and confining himself to telling practical men how to achieve
what they wanted to achieve. Burke's stature as a philosopher
of politics has grown, though not steadily, since his death,
and it has never seemed more impressive than it does today.

As a political philosopher, the key to Burke's influence is
that he has never appeared as the leader of a sect. On the
contrary, he is the Aquinas of British political thought, from
time to time claimed by all the sects but never entirely
harnessed to any; a house of many mansions in which hospi-
tality is generously given on the strict understanding that
guests will be mutually reconciled. In short, in British political thought, Burke is the central point from which heresies
diverge.

So little has a man's temperament to do with his convictions that, to judge from what is known of the life and
character of Edmund Burke, it is almost incredible that he
should have been an apostle of moderation in politics. The
son of an Irish Protestant solicitor and his non-Conformist
wife, he was born in 1729, educated at a Quaker school,
and sent first to Trinity College Dublin and then to the

Temple, where he alienated his father by neglecting his studies. He came to England as a penniless Irish adventurer, and for the rest of his life bore the stigma of those beginnings. Burke's candidature for the admission to the English governing classes was a thousand times bolder than Disraeli's; he was from the first suspected of almost every vice and almost every affiliation which could kill a man's reputation. He was known to be Irish and he was suspected of being a Roman Catholic, a Jesuit in disguise trained at St. Omer, a suspicion which was regarded as proved when in 1756 he married Jane Nugent, the daughter of a Roman Catholic doctor at Bath. He was suspected of being a crook, even within the broad definition of the term admitted by his contemporaries, and what was worse, an unsuccessful and an hypocritical crook, who lost what he had robbed on the Indian Stock market while castigating his political opponents for corruption. Confronted with these suspicions, he was either secretive or angry, but resolutely refused to alter his conduct in any way likely to refute them. Indeed, the whole circumstances of his early life in England were such as to give bad impressions which nothing but several generations of exact scholarship could hope to eradicate.

Of these circumstances, the most distressing were his cousin Will and his younger brother Richard. The fact that they joined him and treated his house as their home until the end of their lives itself made his own debut seem to be merely one act in a concerted campaign of social conquest. Will, who operated in Indian Stock, was beyond doubt extremely dishonest, Richard was merely a wastrel and a cheat at cards. Both of them had an affection and a loyalty for Edmund which called forth a still more fervent and practical response from him, and he not only harboured them but rushed fanatically to their defence whenever, which was most of the time, they were in trouble. To help him with these encumbrances, Burke had only a miserable pittance inherited from his father, and, in his early years, the precarious and negligible rewards of literature, the most constant of which was the small sum he received from Dodsley the printer for editing the *Annual Register* which was founded in 1758 at Burke's initiative. There were, of course, occasional and short-lived strokes of luck. In 1761, for example, Burke was invited to go to Ireland as some sort of unofficial assistant to William Gerard Hamilton, who had himself gone there as secretary to Lord Halifax the Lord Lieutenant. Hamilton benefited immensely from Burke's insight into the Irish question, which was then a compound of the discontents of Catholic tenants with Protestant land-owners, and of Protestant traders with the commercial restrictions imposed by the Home Government; and, in 1763, Burke heard that his reward was to be a pension of £300 a year from the Irish Treasury. Unhappily, the offer was accompanied by the condition that he should cease altogether to write: 'To circumscribe my hopes', expostulated Burke, 'to give up even the possibility of liberty, to annihilate myself for ever!' Burke's first patron was accordingly summarily dismissed. Two years later, there was again a happy turn: Lord Rockingham became Prime Minister, and, over-riding protests against Burke's alleged popery and generally shaky credentials, he made him his private secretary, chiefly, it seems, because he was impressed with the breadth of knowledge which Burke displayed in his annual survey of world affairs for Dodsley. On 26 December 1765, Burke was returned to Parliament for Wendover, partly as a result of the efforts of Will, who was at the time doing well and managed to procure for himself another seat.

One decisive part of the background of Burke's career had yet to be supplied. In 1769 he took a step which has caused unaccountable perplexity in all his biographers: in company with Will and Richard, he bought Gregories, an enormous country estate in Buckinghamshire, for about £25,000, £14,000 of it on mortgage and the rest supplied in loans by friends. It is true that the estate cost well over £2,000 a year to keep up at a time when his annual income was in the hundreds, that it was accordingly a constant source of worry to him until his death, and that even this expenditure could not succeed in expelling an atmosphere of dirt and disorder which caused surprise to such critical guests as Mrs. Thrale, the great literary hostess of Dr. Johnson's circle. Burke knew, however, that the only test which the English governing classes imposes on *parvenus* is that they shall prove themselves capable of successfully living above their incomes for at least the first twenty years of their careers. He was not entirely wrong in his calculation that the best antidote to an obscure origin is a large country house. At the time, his prospects seemed good and in the nature of his circumstances it was on prospects that he must live. Besides all this, the idea of an establishment in the country had a strong appeal to his historical imagination; he enjoyed exercising those virtues and practising that form of life which the English middle classes attribute to the aristocracy. At Beaconsfield, he could give alms to the poor, be a patron of letters (he saved Crabbe from prison) and hold house parties for the eminent. The fact that the imitation was not entirely successful, and in any case was an imitation of nothing real, merely gave it, in the eyes of all but the most complaining of guests, the charm of character. The family, indeed, were a trouble; it was not only the irregularities of Will and Richard, but also the necessity imposed by a generous disposition and adequate house space of entertaining unpresentable Irish relatives for long periods, so that to visit the Burkes in the summer was to get the impression of a rest home for Irish immigrants, and to invite Edmund and Jane back to a party was to expose oneself to an invasion of unpredictable size from England's most troublesome colony. To the imperfections of his relatives, Burke remained throughout his life, valiantly, ostentatiously and most expensively indifferent.

It is necessary to fix Beaconsfield clearly in mind because it was the solace as well as the plague of Burke's life, and, with the affection of his wife Jane, a woman of great tenderness, and later of his son Richard, it supplied, in spite of the mortgage, the most stabilizing influence on a mind otherwise so rent with public cares and passions that it often made even on friends an impression of lunacy. Burke said that when he crossed the threshold of Gregories all worries left him. In the end, it was indeed a source of remorse, for not until after his son Richard's death at the age of thirty-six did he realize the full magnitude of the debts on which his domestic peace was founded, from the knowledge of which Jane and Richard had always shielded him. He began to think of himself as having exploited his wife and robbed his son of his youth and as having been prevented by a harsh fate from doing anything to repay their sacrifice. In his last miserable years, he found the place full of unbearable associations with Richard's memory, yet he clung to it stubbornly, and indeed it was eventually the only place where he could bear to be.

II

The career which was built on Beaconsfield would not have occupied much space in a contemporary *Who's Who*, that invaluable publication in which the offices and attainments of the eminent are listed. Burke was a Member of Parliament from 1759 until 1794, most of the time representing Rotten Boroughs, but also, for six memorable years, the freeholders of Bristol. In Lord Rockingham's brief administration in 1782 he occupied the post of Paymaster General, and he returned to that office in the ill-fated Fox-North Coalition of 1783, after the death of Rockingham had deprived him of his only loyal patron. He never held office again. Thus, he was never more than a junior minister, and even that modest distinction never remained with him more than for a few months on end. The commoner prizes of political service in his day, sinecures, pensions on the civil list and so on, eluded him until three years before his death, when William Pitt, in the face of considerable hostility, made a reasonable provision for him. It is true that the list of Burke's publications would, by virtue of their variety as well as their number, have helped to redeem the impression of mediocrity left by the other entries under his name in the hypothetical *Who's Who* of the day. He would have appeared as the young author of a satire against Bolingbroke under the title of *The Vindication of Natural Society*, a satire so telling as to lose its point entirely by convincing contemporaries that it was by Bolingbroke himself; as a writer of an essay on *The Sublime and the Beautiful* which clarified the current, somewhat vague ideas of psychology as the proper basis for a theory of aesthetics and as the composer of innumerable political pamphlets and tracts including among them the *Reflections on the French Revolution* which was seen by contemporaries as the most eloquent and exhaustive expression of the faith for which England was fighting in the war with the French Revolution and Napoleon.

The bare account of Burke's offices and publications, however, would convey nothing of the impact of his career. It would not show the part which Burke played down to 1782 in welding the Rockinghamite Whigs into something resembling a modern political party, in transforming, that is to say, one of the innumerable splinter groups into which the eighteenth-century House of Commons was divided, into an alliance based on mutual confidence and common principle, disciplined for action in the House of Commons and even, thanks to the literary qualities of Burke, capable of propaganda in the country. It would not reveal the unparalleled combination of fervour and detailed industry which Burke put into the campaign for reducing the Royal influence in the House of Commons, and over elections to it, by curtailing the patronage at the King's disposal; it would say nothing of the fierce and imperishable campaign which Burke led against the policy of trying to coerce the American colonies or of one of the greatest dramas in British parliamentary history, the impeachment of Warren

Hastings for crimes and misdemeanours in the government of India, in which Burke was chief prosecuting counsel for the House of Lords for fourteen years. Even the contemporary success of the *Reflections* gives no clue to Burke's importance, for, according to the judgement of his own age, that tract was chiefly a magnificent piece of war-time literature. Not till much later did it come to be acknowledged as the nearest approach to an accurate definition of whatever common political philosophy the English have.

Above all, no bare recital of the events of Burke's career can do justice to the impression he made on those who watched him. Here was this Irish *parvenu*, suddenly thrust, so to speak, into the 'Royal Enclosure' of late eighteenth-century British politics, with a hoard of doubtful or at the best scruffy relations in train, directing a series of political campaigns which cut to the foundations of government and empire, and thereby put an end to that preoccupation with minute particularities which had distinguished English public life ever since the Jacobite danger was expelled in 1745.

'An Irishman about five feet ten inches in height and fifty years of age; wearing a tight brown coat and a little bob-wig with curls; near-sighted, so that as he spoke, you might mark an occasional working of the brow, as you would also notice a beaky nose and a tight-pursed mouth; often harsh in tone and violent in gesticulation, and always speaking with much of the Irish accent and "an habitual undulating motion of the head . . . which had the appearance of indicating something of a self-confident or intractable spirit"; an Irishman you might have thought to be a schoolmaster if you had not known in advance that he was the Chrysostom of English politics . . .' Thus vividly Sir Ernest Barker recaptures the effect which Burke made on his Bristol constituents. It was not altogether appetizing. Among the eminent men of the day Burke had, indeed, fervent admirers, most notably Dr. Johnson. He was a conversational genius. His mind was shaped by the most valuable of all intellectual experiences, prolonged and undisciplined reading; he was sunk in history, in the classics and in the Bible. What he took in was not merely stored ready to be produced whenever the exigencies of debate or discussion required an epigram or an allusion; on the contrary, it supplied the material for a massive and powerful intellect, always under the sway of some consuming purpose, to weld into argument, and usually argument directed to some purpose no less comprehensive at the very least than the salvation of the State. He was equally capable, of course, of playing the part required of all his distinguished contemporaries, that of perpetual brains 'trustee' to Boswell and in that capacity of giving impromptu opinions on such matters as the relative merits of double and single beds in marriage; but, though the vivacity and conviction with which Burke talked prevented him from ever being a bore, there is no evidence (for that cited by Boswell will not do) for the view that he had a sense of humour. He would wind himself into a subject whether in the drawing-room or on the floor of the house, thinking, worrying, qualifying as he went, until all this cautious, circuitous meditation yielded a conclusion, a conclusion exquisite in its balance, but, because of the very patience with which it had been wrought, devastating in its effect. Women fainted when they heard him impeaching Hastings, and feared that like Chatham he would die from the force of his own eloquence. He had the sort of fanaticism which distinguishes men who are not only moderate by conviction but moderate from the subtlety of their minds and the sensibility of their hearts, and who cherish moderation so much that they are overpowered with anger, pity and terror when it is assailed.

Add these qualities to the perpetual strain created by the suspicion of his origins, to the necessary unpopularity of many of his causes, to the defiant, unworldly magnanimity which made it impossible for him to betray a friend even when his friendship had become a taint in the eyes of others, and it is not hard to see why he never got Cabinet office. The reason had nothing to do with the alleged defects of intellectuals—coldness, inability to get on with people, the reticence of pride—none of these qualities has ever prevented a man from being Prime Minister of England—the reasons for Burke's professional failure were totally different. Given the confidence of others he could be a brilliant party manager as he showed under Rockingham; but his prophetic anger was too great to make it easy for opponents to be reconciled with him: and since his course involved, without inconsistency, first the alienation of the Tories and then the alienation of the Whig admirers of the French Revolution, this was a serious defect. It was rendered fatal by the apparent doubtfulness of his credentials, which was always ready to the hands of his opponents. His response to their jeers and calumnies was of course often at fault, as in such cases it always must be: he was by turns haughtily indifferent and ferociously angry, but had he been by any ordinary standards a peevish and petulant character he could never have remained at the heart of British politics for thirty-five years. Only a little well-intentioned effort with some prospect of reward for compliance would have been needed in happier circumstances to contain his passion within the limits of what can be endured at Westminster. He had the misfortune of commanding an infinite and minute mastery of detail (exhibited particularly in his reports on India, his impeachment of Hastings, and his proposals for reforming the public economy) with an unrivalled grasp of principle; mediocrity is disturbed by principle but humiliated by detail; Burke's talents could have been much more tactfully disposed. As it was he had a prophet's reward, and his last years in Parliament were a period during which baiting Burke became one of the commonest diversions of the House. Beaconsfield was the only refuge.

III

It is tolerable not to get office; it is not easy to bear the continual rejection of one's counsel. It is scarcely too much to say that each of the great practical aims of Burke's career appear to have been frustrated in his lifetime, a burden which cannot have been much lightened by the success of the *Reflections on the French Revolution* or even by a constant reputation among the best minds of the day for genius unequalled by anyone else in politics. To begin with Burke set out to abolish the corruption of the constitution by Royal patronage, a theme pursued in his pamphlet *Thoughts on the Causes of the Present Discontents*. Burke gave the cause literary immortality, but his handling of it was a practical failure. The demand for a wider electoral franchise or at any rate a more rational one had already been heard; but Burke was against mechanical adjustments, believing that if the results of the great Revolution settlement of 1688 could be defended against the encroachments of the Crown which now bribed the Parliament it could no longer defy, the constitution would appear again in its historic perfection. Royal patronage was not abolished or substantially curtailed; instead the King gave the country a Prime Minister, the younger Pitt, whom it was possible until the middle of the twentieth century to describe without qualifying clauses as the greatest she has ever had; in the end the purification of the constitution, if so it must be deemed, was brought about by the very methods which Burke had rejected, that is to say, by widening the franchise and making it more uniform. Burke sought to reform the government of India and to impeach Warren Hastings as the arch representative of the cruelty and corruption which disfigured the government of India as then conducted by the chartered East India Company. The India Bill which he drafted for the Fox-North Coalition merely led to the defeat of the Coalition. The fourteen years spent in accusing Warren Hastings before the House of Lords according to the procedure known as impeachment (by which the lower House was empowered to bring servants of the Crown before the House of Lords to answer for misconduct), ended in Hastings' acquittal. Burke tried in one of the two greatest battles of his career to stop the Government from driving the American colonies into rebellion by insisting to the full legal limit on the right to tax them, and then he tried to bring about conciliation with them; the War of Independence was not averted, but ended in Britain's defeat, and in a rupture between two English speaking peoples the full significance of which for the destiny of mankind intrigues and terrifies the imagination. It is true that the English eventually took up arms against the French Revolution, long after Burke had pleaded for intervention; what however drew them into the war was not the eloquence of Burke but the invasion of the Low Countries, to which Britain's reaction was fore-ordained by history and geography. The impression of wasted effort and passion spent without fruit which would have been left on any but a veritable knight of faith by this unmitigated record of rejected advice, was crippling, and at the end, which came on 9 July 1797, Burke was almost crippled by it.

It would be satisfactory to add that on all these practical questions posterity had confirmed Burke's views: but judgements like this are usually superficial, and, on many points, the reverse may be said. There has been a reaction against what is commonly called 'Whig history', against the view of English constitutional development which treats the Crown as the invariable enemy and the Parliament as the constant friend of the people. Any undergraduate who has read Sir Lewis Namier now realizes that the institutions which Burke defended were as corrupt as the practices which he assailed; that whereas he minded the King giving sinecure posts he did not mind the aristocracy having Rotten Boroughs; that the effect of his reforms would not have been so much to purge the constitution as to destroy its inner balance by confirming the ascendancy of the aristocracy which, freed from Royal competition, would have been able to run Parliament to its own satisfaction. Everyone now knows that Lord North was not so feeble or so foolish as the picture presented by Burke suggests, and that the arguments over American independence were not all on one side, a point which, it should be added does not invalidate Burke's main point that the attempt to tax the colonies by force was inexpedient. Certainly, Burke's remedies for India, regarded as administrative proposals, had little influence on the slow development of an honourable British government there in the nineteenth century. It may be doubted whether earlier British interference in Europe against the French Revolution would have been wise, and it would certainly not have been in keeping with Britain's diplomatic tradition.

It is clear, therefore, that the greatness of Burke is to be sought somewhere else than in the invariable correctness of his own specific remedies for the discontents of the day. What has been claimed for him is that from all these speeches and writings there emerges a political philosophy, a complex philosophy incapable of being easily reduced to abstract expression, but none the less a coherent philosophy, and one which has had a unique part in shaping British political practice. Added to this is the incontestable claim that Burke was a great master of the written and spoken word, certainly a model for orators, but possibly also a master of elegant and exact writing.

IV

Before Burke emerged into politics, he had written two books, one of which bears only indirectly on politics while the other has nothing to do with that subject; but both of them give some indication of the contribution he was to make to political philosophy. The satire on Bolingbroke, *The Vindication of Natural Society*, has all the appearance of a political tract even when its satirical intention is understood, but in reality it was an attack on Bolingbroke's religious opinions. Bolingbroke, a sceptic, had left for posthumous publication an assault on the whole idea of revealed religion and a defence for an alternative basis for moral judgement, that is to say, natural religion or the religion of reason. Burke's method of refuting him was to transfer the argument to the plane of politics, and, posing as Bolingbroke, to take the artificial arrangements of society as the equivalent of revealed religion, and the political principles arising directly from reason as the equivalence of natural religion. If revealed religion, so he argued, was a compound of traditions founded upon accident and hallowed by superstition and prejudice, so was the whole mechanism of civil society. If we were to embrace reason as the only guide to religious truth, so we must embrace reason as the only guide to political behaviour. To do this is to condemn outright the arrangements of all known societies, to discredit all the methods by which society is kept together, to unleash universal chaos and thus 'to vindicate ourselves into perfect liberty'. It may be possible to have more than one opinion about the logic of this exercise of Burke's in reducing Bolingbroke to absurdity by transplanting his principles from religion to politics; the point is that Burke's purpose was not to vindicate artificial society by satirizing the notion of natural society, but to vindicate revealed religion by satirizing the notion of natural religion. The assumption upon which the whole effect rests is that application of naked reason to the conduct of politics would produce disruption, and that this fact is in itself enough to refute the sovereignty of pure reason in politics. Burke took these propositions for granted; in them appears the germ of the great Burkian doctrine that prejudice, far from being the enemy of social good, provides the foundation and the motive power of every society; that without it social life would be as impossible as physical life would be if the act of breathing were always to require a conscious exercise of the rational will. In it also appears the germ of another idea which interpreters of Burke have often been apt to misunderstand, the idea that faith in tradition rests largely and legitimately on scepticism of the dependability of men's private reasoning. Later these doctrines will develop into something of massive intellectual power; at this time in Burke's career they are merely taken for granted.

The second of Burke's pre-political treatises, that *On the Sublime and Beautiful*, never deeply influenced aesthetic theory in England but had a profound influence on Kant and much nineteenth-century German thought. Here, it is characteristic of Burke that he should have followed Shaftesbury, Addison, and others in deploring the habit of trying to discover the nature of beauty by studying beautiful objects, instead of by studying, with the aid of the best available psychological methods, the sentiments to which these objects appeal. Experience was the basis of his aesthetics as it was to be of his politics.

A conviction of the destructive effects of the application of pure reason to human affairs, of the utility of prejudice and of the importance of experiment and the observation of experience in the making of judgements, these were the starting-points of Burke's political thought. That thought was expressed in a series of contributions to debates about matters which, far from being speculative, put in immediate question the survival of the country and the Empire. The two greatest events of Burke's life-time were also decisive for the whole course of modern history: they were the American War of Independence and the French Revolution. To use the jargon from which it is impossible altogether to free the discussion of politics, Burke's reaction to the first was liberal and to the second conservative. These two contributions of Burke's, though they may have occupied less of his time than did the affairs of India, contain the essence of his political beliefs. The test of whether he had a consistent political philosophy depends largely whether it is thought possible to reconcile them with each other.

V

The controversies leading to the War of Independence give an extraordinarily clear picture of the main divisions over the principles of politics in late eighteenth-century England and America. The imposition of a Stamp Duty by the English Government raised the purely legal question of whether the Parliament at Westminster was empowered to impose direct taxation on the colonies. This question was put shortly after the doctrine of parliamentary sovereignty dating from the sixteenth century had been given its most vigorous and systematic expression in the writing of Blackstone. When the Stamp Duty was withdrawn in deference to American protests, and an attempt made to raise the necessary revenue by new duties on American trade, the colonists shifted their ground, claiming that the home government had no right to impose even indirect taxation except for the purpose of regulating trade as distinct from raising money. Soon the furies of fundamentalism were to be unleashed, the English government took its stand on the principle of sovereignty, and this, not in the comparatively prosaic form in which that principle was later to be enunciated by the Benthamite jurist Austin, but on the *a priori* grounds of Blackstone; soon the Americans were founding their case on the opposite dogma of natural rights. Constitutional Whigs like Chatham and Camden, who derived their ideas from the conflicts of seventeenth-century England, took their stand on the doctrine of a historic fundamental law which limited, by custom and originally by divine ordinance, the spheres of the various organs of government and therefore made sovereignty impossible. Burke's great contribution to this debate was to contribute a principle wholly different from that of any of these parties, the principle of utility based on historic empiricism.

It is worth while to analyse in detail the great speech which he delivered in the House of Commons on 22 March 1775, on moving his resolutions for conciliation with the colonies. Burke begins, after some formal courtesies designed to excuse his presumption in addressing the House at such length and at the same time to illustrate the superior consistency of his opinions, with an exposition of the nature and

principles of the scheme he was proposing: 'The proposi-
tion,' he cried, 'is peace.' England must take the initiative
in offering terms of reconciliation; this suggests two questions, the first of which is whether England ought to make
concessions to the colonists, since reconciliation will be
impossible without concession. Before this question is
answered, Burke argues, 'it is necessary to consider dis-
tinctly the true nature and the peculiar circumstances of the
object we have before us'. We must govern America according to the circumstances which history and geography have
created, 'not according to our own imaginations; not according to abstract ideas of right; by no means according to mere
general themes of government, the resort to which appears
to me, in our present situation, no better than arrant
trifling'.

Accordingly Burke sets out to give a detailed analysis of
all the circumstances of the American colonies and their
relationship to the mother country. The first thing, he
mildly observes to a House now fully accustomed to debat-
ing the law and the metaphysics of the situation, is to consider how many people there are in the American colonies.
He describes at length the growing size of the colonies,
which increases so rapidly that while we are 'deliberating
on the mode of governing two millions, we shall find we
have millions more to manage'. This is necessary in order
to set the question in perspective, since the current assumption
was that the American colonies were an unruly dependency;
the mere contemplation of their size and potential power
warned England, according to Burke, against trifling 'with
so large a mass of the interests and feelings of the human
race'. This is a theme which appeals strongly to Burke's
imagination and evokes from him one of the most impressive
passages in his work:

> It is good for us to be here. We stand where we have an immense
> view of what is, and what is past. Clouds, indeed, and darkness rest
> upon the future. Let us, however, before we descend from this noble
> eminence reflect that this growth of our national prosperity has

happened within the short period of the life of man. It has happened
within 68 years. There are those alive whose memory might touch
the two extremities. For instance My Lord Bathurst might remem-
ber all the stages of the progress.

Burke goes on to imagine an angel unfolding to Bathurst as
a child the future of the American colonies:

> Young man, there is America—which this day serves for little
> more than to amuse you with stories of savage man, and uncouth
> manners; yet shall, before you taste of death, show itself equal to
> the whole of that commerce which now attracts the envy of the
> world. Whatever England has been growing to by a progressive
> increase of improvement, brought in by varieties of people, by
> succession of civilizing conquests and civilizing settlements in a
> series of 1700 years, you shall see as much added to her by America
> in the course of a single life.

Burke reflects that, for the child Bathurst to believe such a
prophecy would have required 'all the sanguine incredulity
of youth, and all the fervid glow of enthusiasm'. But 'Fortunate man, he has lived to see it! Fortunate indeed, if he
lives to see nothing that shall vary the prospect, and cloud
the setting of his day!'
There follows a digression on the general futility of force:

> America, gentlemen say, is a noble object. It is an object well worth
> fighting for. Certainly it is, if fighting were the best way of gaining
> them . . . My opinion is much more in favour of prudent manage-
> ment, than of force; considering force not as an odious, but a feeble
> instrument, for preserving a people so numerous, so active, so grow-
> ing, so spirited as this, in a profitable and subordinate connexion
> with us. [Burke continues:] A further objection to force is, that you
> *impair the object* by your very endeavours to preserve it. The thing
> you fight for is not the thing which you recover; but depreciated,
> sunk, wasted, and consumed in the contest.

He now resumes his analysis of the circumstances of
America, turning to the American character. It has inherited
an unusual devotion to liberty from the fact of the original

settlers' having been Puritans fleeing from a hostile government. In the South, where the Episcopal Church was strong, the submissiveness which this religious background might be expected to enjoy was entirely offset by the institution of slavery, for no one, Burke penetratingly observes, is harder to control than the master of a slave. Then, he draws attention to the circumstance that the study of Law was more popular in eighteenth-century America than in any other part of the world, and lawyers are by nature jealous of rights, not merely resenting oppression in fact but resenting it even in principle; finally with a grand touch of contempt which must delight the heart of every political realist, he patiently reminds his colleagues in the House of Commons that 'three thousand miles of ocean lie between you and them . . . seas roll, and months pass, between the order and the execution; and the want of a speedy explanation of a single point is enough to defeat a whole system'.

The analysis leads Burke to put the question, ignored by all the other participants in the debate, of how in fact you were to deal with such a people: there are three conceivable courses: to try and alter the conditions by restricting the growth of America; but, if the Government stopped its grants of land what would the consequence be? 'The people would occupy without grants'; if the Government tried to abate the high aristocratic state of Virginia, as some suggested it should, by declaring a general enfranchisement of their slaves, it would be necessary to induce the slaves to be freed, and 'it is sometimes as hard to persuade slaves to be free as it is to compel freemen to be slaves; and in this auspicious scheme, we should have both these pleasing tasks on our hands at once'. The second alternative, coercion, is again reviewed and dismissed for the reasons already implied in the analysis of the American character. There remains Burke's own policy, that of concession, or, as opponents of a later day would have dubbed it, 'appeasement': the main objection levelled against it is that it would involve abandoning the right of taxation inherent in a sovereign; then comes what to contemporaries was the most astonishing of all Burke's precepts:

> Sir, I think you must perceive, that I am resolved this day to have nothing at all to do with the question of the right of taxation. Some gentlemen startle—but it is true; . . . I do not examine, whether the giving away a man's money be a power excepted and reserved out of the general trust of government; and how far all mankind, in all forms of polity, are entitled to an exercise of that right by the charter of nature. Or whether, on the contrary, a right of taxation is necessarily involved in the general principle of legislation, and inseparable from the ordinary supreme power . . . High and reverend authorities lift up their heads on both sides; and there is no sure footing in the middle . . . I do not intend to be overwhelmed in that bog, though in such respectable company. The question with me is, not whether you have a right to render your people miserable; but whether it is not your interest to make them happy.

Burke goes on to ask what light English experience throws on the problem of the colonies. He takes the pacification of Ireland, or its relative pacification, that of Wales and of the palatinates of Chester and Durham as instances of the proven value of the policy of reconciliation. He concludes with six propositions which do no more than state the undisputed facts of the case, but which, without artifice, make the three resolutions embodying his plan of conciliation appear irresistible.

This ranks as the greatest speech of Burke's career. At the time it won unbounded admiration from his friends, particularly from Charles James Fox, and inspired respect in his foes. It was described by Lord Morley, the great Liberal philosopher-statesman, who wrote Burke's life a century later, as an indispensable part of any man's instruction in statecraft, and as probably the greatest manifesto of the principles of liberal statesmanship ever produced. Lord Morley was a Radical, who, though the fact is scarcely remembered, resigned from Asquith's administration on the eve of the 1914 struggle rather than commit his country to what he regarded as the folly and futility of a modern war. It is a remarkable fact that such a man as Morley should see

in Edmund Burke, now commonly thought of as the philosopher of Conservatism, the source of so much Liberal
wisdom. Indeed, the explanation is that he was thinking of
what used to be called the early Burke, on the assumption,
though Morley was himself too percipient to make it con-
sciously, that the French Revolution was a dividing line in
Burke's life as it was in Wordsworth's. He could see Burke's
speech on American conciliation, with some justice, as
the charter of the self-governing Empire. It was, in truth,
the inspiration of the Quebec Constitution of 1792, and the
general principles of Burke's colonial policy may be said
to have governed Britain's policy towards her white subjects
abroad ever afterwards, a strange irony in view of the dis-
proportionate time which Burke gave to the affairs of India,
and the elaboration of schemes for that country's welfare
which have had no discernible influence on its future.

What matters, however, to a consideration of the consistency of Burke's thought, is the political doctrine which
emerges from the speech. It is not merely a guide to practical
statesmanship; it contains some at least of the essentials of a
philosophy of politics. Those who are determined to dissect
can distinguish at least five major principles of general application in this magnificent exercise of the art of political
analysis. There is, first and foremost, the principle of utility,
the theory that no consideration of abstract right can be a
sufficient basis for just authority and just obedience, but that
the proper end of government is the happiness of its subjects,
and that this should be the sovereign guide to its conduct,
determining how far it shall press its authority in practice.
Secondly, there is the principle that a nation's character is
the product of its history and geography, a principle to
which systematic expression had been given by Montesquieu
in his *L'Esprit des Lois*, but so thoroughly assimilated by
Burke that his elaborate enumeration of the circumstances
which determine the American character would rank today
as what is odiously called 'geo-politics'. Thirdly, there is
the germ, in a much modified form, of a doctrine very

fashionable in eighteenth-century England, which took it from eighteenth-century France, that of the automatic harmony of interests. In Burke it assumes no more dogmatic form than the assertion that the view that force can accomplish everything is false; and that, on the contrary, a country may often best promote its interests in the long run by curbing its ambitions in the short run. Fourthly, there is the appeal to experience, the plea for a reverent consideration not of legal precedents but of the moral and political convictions of our ancestors. Lastly, and closely associated with it, the appeal to experiment, to the view that the consequences of action in politics are always so complex that every possible guide should be sought from history.

VI

Burke's *Reflections on the French Revolution* was first published in November 1790, while opinion in England was still divided on the merits of the revolutionary cause; it was repeatedly republished and indeed was largely responsible for rallying English opinion, though it was not the decisive step which Burke would have wished it to be towards converting England to the need for military intervention. It was subsequently much lengthened, and in its final form, though every sentence bears the mark of having been deliberately forged for a purpose, it has not the economy and logical sequence of the speech on American conciliation. It is full of honest passion, and inspired by Burke's characteristic conviction that it is the duty of a man not to be deaf to the counsels of the heart but to submit them to the judgement of prudence. For these reasons, it cannot be easily summarized. The form preserved throughout is that of a letter to a young Frenchman, and this also gives Burke a latitude more fitting to his purpose of writing a political pamphlet than to that of scholars trying to distil from it a doctrine

of politics. The argument starts with a comparison of the
doctrines of the English revolution of 1688 with those of
the French Revolution, a comparison arising from Burke's
resentment of a sermon preached by Dr. Price, the Minister
of the Old Jewry, in which the two were treated as parallels,
and by the various pronouncements of the Constitutional
Society and the Revolution Society in England. From this,
Burke proceeds to launch his attack on the French National
Assembly, and to contrast the régime which it is trying to
establish with the established political and social order in
England. The book contains an elaborate account of the
various elements in the pre-revolutionary constitution of
France and in its social structure, and ends with a more
detailed and full-scale denunciation of the Assembly.

Burke, it must be remembered, is for the purposes of this
pamphlet looking at the French Revolution with the eyes
of a Frenchman, not, as he was looking at the American
Revolution, with the eyes of an Imperial statesman concerned to maintain a threatened link in the Empire; in the
case of America, the question is how should authority anti-
cipate and react to a serious challenge; in the case of France,
the question is what are the principles by which a state
should be reformed. A precise parallel would only be
possible if Burke had set out to advise Louis XVI in 1788
on how to cope with an impending revolution, and this he
never did.

To those in search of Burke's political philosophy, certain
passages in the *Reflections* stand out luminously. The starting
point of the analysis must be the comparison of the proceed-
ings of the English revolutionists in 1688 with that of the
French revolutionaries of 1789. The English revolutionists
set out to improve the State by correcting its corruptions,
they sought diligently to preserve whatever they were not
absolutely compelled to destroy in order to accomplish that
reform; when they departed from precedent they did so
with reluctance, and whenever they created something new
they tried to gain for it the respect due to age by absorbing

it in their national tradition. The French might have followed their example:

> Your privileges, though discontinued, were not lost to memory. Your constitution, it is true, whilst you were out of possession, had suffered waste and dilapidation, but you possessed in some parts the walls and in all the foundations of a noble and venerable castle. You might have repaired those walls; you might have built on those old foundations.

Instead, the French had chosen to assert abstract principles professing to be universally valid, and to set up their own reasons as superior to the reason of antiquity.

rationalism

Burke, thus, is principally concerned to attack what later became known as Rationalism in politics, and to oppose to it the method of gradual improvement based on the careful garnering of experience: 'They wrought underground a mine that will blow up at one grand explosion all examples of antiquity, all precedents, charters, and acts of parliament. They have the "rights of men" . . . against these no agreement is binding.'

Burke then asks whether he is committed, by this enmity to Rationalism in politics to deny altogether the appeal to natural right, and he finds that he is not: 'In denying their false claims of right, I do not mean to injure those which are real, and are such as their pretended rights would totally destroy. If civil society be made for the advantage of man, all the advantages for which it is made become his right.' The test is always the same, that which conduces to the welfare of society is a human right: 'Government is a contrivance of human wisdom to provide for human wants.' To provide for human wants effectively, government must bridle human passions, and, 'in this sense the restraints on men, as well as their liberties, are to be reckoned among their rights'.

The necessary restraints, like the liberties themselves, admit of infinite modifications, 'they cannot be settled upon any abstract rule; and nothing is so foolish as to discuss them upon that principle'.

This does not mean, however, that reason has no part in determining human rights, or that human rights have no element of constancy in them but are merely makeshifts of convenience: 'These metaphysic rights entering into common life, like rays of light which pierce into a dense medium, are, by the laws of nature, refracted from their straight line.' Man's nature is infinitely complex and various, and his institutions must express this complexity and variety.

Burke returns to the English constitution founded upon Church, Crown, nobles and commons, and from his analysis of it draws two principles, the principle of organic growth re-expressed in terms of an adaptation of the theory of social contract, and the principle of balance between contending interests.

> Society is indeed a contract. Subordinate contracts for objects of mere occasional interest may be dissolved at pleasure—but the State ought not to be considered nothing better than a partnership agreement in a trade of pepper and coffee, calico or tobacco, or some other such low concern, to be taken up for a little temporary interest and to be dissolved by the fancy of the parties. It is to be looked on with other reverence; because it is not a partnership in things subservient only to the gross animal existence of a temporary and perishable nature. It is a partnership in all science; a partnership in all art; a partnership in every virtue and in all perfection . . . It becomes a partnership between not only those who are living, but between those who are living, those who are dead, and those who are yet to be born.

And the people he defines as a sum total of all the separate orders and interests of society; when all these orders and interests act together in harmony (and this is only rarely so, because their natural condition is one of wholesome ten- Hobbes sion), 'When great multitudes act together, under that discipline of nature, I recognize the people'.

Even at the time of his bitterest enmity towards the Revolution, Burke never abandoned the view that great mass movements, however misguided, cannot be treated with mere contempt; his thoughts on the French constitutions concludes with this passage:

> The evil is stated, in my opinion, as it exists. The remedy must be where power, wisdom, and information, I hope, are more united with good intentions than they can be with me. I have done with this subject, I believe, for ever. It has given me many anxious moments for the two last years. If a great change is to be made in human affairs, the minds of men will be fitted to it, the general opinions and feelings will draw that way. Every fear, every hope, will forward it; and then they, who persist in opposing this mighty current in human affairs, will appear rather to resist the decrees of Providence itself, than the mere designs of men. They will not be resolute and firm but perverse and obstinate.

The real vice of the revolutionaries, Burke continually repeats, is the presumptuous demand for simplicity which leads them to renounce the past, to break up all the solid links that hold society together, and to undermine the prejudices and conventions which are the basis of its daily intercourse without examining the reasons behind them. Burke believes that one of the main danger points in this revolutionary process is the weakening of those lesser associations out of which society is formed and which are its cement.

> To be attached to the subdivision, to love the little platoon we belong to in society, is the first principle (the germ as it were) of public affections. It is the first link in the series by which we proceed towards a love to our country, and to mankind. The interest of that portion of social arrangement is a trust in the hands of all those who compose it; and as none but bad men would justify it in abuse, none but traitors would barter it away for their own personal advantage.

The presumption of the revolutionaries is certain to fail, because it is a mere doctrine of naked force; this passion for abstract equality will end in tyranny, 'the person who really commands the army is your master; the master . . . of your king, the master of your assembly, the master of your whole republic'. In the career of Napoleon, Burke's prophecy was fulfilled to the letter.

VII

Recall the different circumstances of the two pronouncements, and it is clear that Burke on America and Burke on France are essentially the same. The appeal to utility, the appeal to experiment, the appeal to experience, the futility of force employed for any but limited and clearly defined ends, are common to both. The difference is that in the *Reflections* they have received a more deliberate and majestic expression, at times so majestic as to give an impression of political mysticism which deluded many German admirers into believing that he anticipated Hegel. In reality, Burke says in both pronouncements what he implied in everything else he wrote and said in his career, that sound political judgements are not to be made by employing only one faculty or appealing to only one intellectual authority but are complex, resting on an appeal to reason, checked by tradition and checked again by the carefully observed results of contemporary experience. He asks us to respect the past, not merely out of deference to the wisdom of our ancestry but also from doubt of our own private stock of wisdom; he asks us to respect tradition not on the mystical ground that tradition is the voice of the people but largely on the practical ground that however bad a tradition may be in proportion as it has shaped character it has provided the material out of which alone reformed institutions can be forged. In the *Reflections on the French Revolution* there occurs this lucid piece of common sense regarding the nature and function of prejudice in politics:

> Many of our men of speculation, instead of exploding general prejudices, employ their sagacity to discover the latent wisdom which prevails in them. If they find what they seek, and they seldom fail, they think it more wise to continue the prejudice, with the reason involved, than to cast away the coat of prejudice, and to leave nothing but the naked reason; because prejudice, with its reason, has a motive to give action to that reason, and an affection

which will give it permanence. Prejudice is of ready application in
the emergency; it previously engages the mind in a steady course
of wisdom and virtue, and does not leave the man hesitating in the
moment of decision, sceptical, puzzled, and unresolved. Prejudice
renders a man's virtue his habit; and not a series of unconnected
acts. Through just prejudice, his duty becomes a part of his nature.

Burke is prevented from being a doctrinaire Conservative
by this English quality of doubt; he is the greatest of the
English political philosophers of moderation in the line of
Hooker, the apologist of the English reformation, Halifax
the Trimmer, and the great Marquis of Salisbury. But he is
not the possession of a political party. The British political
system rests on the challenge and response of radicalism and
Conservatism; it is part of the essence of a radical that he uses
the language of dogmatism in politics and sounds like the
people whom Burke condemned, but it is also part of the
essense of an English radical that he in practice recognizes
that his utopia will not be fulfilled in the form in which he
has conceived it, that he is contributing to a settlement of
affairs which transcends the views of both Right and Left.
Today this sceptical and empirical approach to politics is
again being recognized by the English-speaking peoples as
having the stature of a philosophy, and Burke has never
enjoyed so prominent a place in the esteem of the academies.

In one outstanding respect, Burke does not shed much
direct light on contemporary politics: the politics of the late
eighteenth century were not much preoccupied with the
struggle between capital and labour, for capitalism was
scarcely born. Burke's views on the position of the poor in
society accordingly are easy to dismiss as hypocrisy now:

> They must labour to obtain what by labour can be obtained; and
> when they find, as they commonly do, the success disproportioned
> to the endeavour, they must be taught their consolation in the final
> proportions of eternal justice. Of this consolation whoever deprives
> them deadens their industry, and strikes at the root of all acquisition
> as of all conservation.

Yet even here, Burke's teaching has its contemporary relevance: there is even in the atomic age a recurring gap between man's ambitions and his power to satisfy them, and the need for a principle which will reconcile him to his limitations is as great as ever.

'Ned', his cousin Will once remarked, using the measure of patriotism which occurred most easily to him, 'works as hard as if he were getting 12 per cent from the Empire.' Burke may have been disposed to ask on his deathbed what all the striving of this turbulent career had produced: the answer of posterity, at least in posterity's present mood, must be: the nearest approach to an exact and comprehensive definition of the total contribution of the English-speaking peoples to the common stock of human wisdom about politics.

EDMUND BURKE

A Select Bibliography

(Place of publication London unless stated otherwise)

Bibliography:

Note: Burke's bibliography is unusually complicated and a definitive canon and a correct text of his writings have yet to be established. The solution of these problems, evolving the identification of the number, sequence and revision of numerous editions, must await the Bibliography now being prepared by Dr. W. A. Todd of Harvard. The short-title list in the *Cambridge Bibliography of English Literature*, though the fullest at present available, fails among other things to record a number of books entirely by Burke, or to which he contributed, and 17 authorized editions (as well as some 120 reprints). Burke's papers, formerly at Wentworth Woodhouse, are now available for research at Sheffield University.

Collected Works:

THE WORKS, edited by F. Laurence and W. King [Burke's literary executors]. 8 vols. (1792–1827).

Later editions, published in London and Boston up to the end of the century, are variously in 16, 12, 9 and 8 volumes. The text, though often incorrect, has been used for all subsequent reprints of Burke's writings.

THE WORKS, edited by W. Willis and F. W. Raffety. 6 vols. (1906–7). In the World's Classics.

CORRESPONDENCE 1744–1797, edited by Earl Fitzwilliam and Sir R. Bourke. 4 vols. (1844).

Note: The definitive edition of Burke's Correspondence, edited by Professor T. W. Copeland and Dr. R. A. Smith, is in active preparation.

Selected Works:

SELECT WORKS, edited by E. J. Payne. 3 vols. Oxford (1874–8).

SPEECHES AND LETTERS ON AMERICAN AFFAIRS, edited by P. McKevitt (1908). In Everyman's Library.

MAXIMS AND REFLECTIONS, edited by F. W. Raffety (1915).

SELECT SPEECHES AND LETTERS, edited by W. Morison. Cambridge (1920).

SELECTIONS AND EXTRACTS, edited by A. M. D. Hughes. Oxford (1921). With essays by Hazlitt, Arnold and others.

LETTERS, Mainly Political, edited by H. Laski (1922). In the World's Classics.

SELECTIONS, edited by L. N. Broughton. New York (1925).

SELECTED PROSE, edited by P. Magnus (1948).

Separate Works:

A VINDICATION OF NATURAL SOCIETY (1756).

A PHILOSOPHICAL ENQUIRY INTO THE ORIGIN OF OUR IDEAS OF THE SUBLIME AND BEAUTIFUL (1757).

AN ESSAY TOWARDS AN ABRIDGMENT OF THE ENGLISH HISTORY [1757].

[AN ACCOUNT OF THE EUROPEAN SETTLEMENTS IN AMERICA. 2 vols. (1757).] By William Burke, but revised and contributed to by his kinsman Edmund Burke.

AN EXAMINATION OF THE COMMERCIAL PRINCIPLES OF THE LATE NEGOTIATIONS BETWEEN GREAT BRITAIN AND FRANCE IN 1761 (1762).

A SHORT ACCOUNT OF A LATE SHORT ADMINISTRATION (1766).

OBSERVATIONS ON A LATE PUBLICATION INTITULED 'THE PRESENT STATE OF THE NATION' (1769).

THOUGHTS ON THE CAUSE OF THE PRESENT DISCONTENTS (1770).

SPEECH . . . ON AMERICAN TAXATION. Bristol [1774].

SPEECHES AT HIS ARRIVAL AT BRISTOL AND AT THE CONCLUSION OF THE POLL (1774).

THE SPEECH . . . ON MOVING HIS RESOLUTIONS FOR CONCILIATION WITH THE COLONIES (1775).

A LETTER TO . . . THE SHERIFFS OF [BRISTOL] ON THE AFFAIRS OF AMERICA (1777).

TWO LETTERS . . . TO GENTLEMEN IN THE CITY OF BRISTOL ON IRELAND (1778).

SUBSTANCE OF THE SPEECHES . . . ON MR. BURKE'S GIVING NOTICE OF HIS INTENTION TO BRING IN A BILL FOR THE RETRENCHMENT OF PUBLIC EXPENCES (1779).

SPEECH . . . ON PRESENTING A PLAN . . . FOR THE BETTER SECURITY OF THE INDEPENDENCE OF PARLIAMENT (1780).

A LETTER . . . IN VINDICATION OF HIS CONDUCT WITH REGARD TO THE AFFAIRS OF IRELAND. Dublin (1780).

SPEECH . . . IN BRISTOL UPON HIS PARLIAMENTARY CONDUCT (1780).

LETTER TO A PEER OF IRELAND ON THE PENAL LAWS (1782).

SPEECH . . . ON REFORM IN THE HOUSE OF COMMONS (1782).

SPEECH . . . UPON MR. FOX'S EAST INDIA BILL (1784).

SPEECH . . . RELATIVE TO THE NABOB OF ARCOT'S DEBTS (1785).

ARTICLES OF CHARGE . . . AGAINST WARREN HASTINGS (1786).

SPEECH IN OPENING THE IMPEACHMENT OF WARREN HASTINGS (1788).

REFLECTIONS ON THE REVOLUTION IN FRANCE (1790).
A definitive recension of the text of this famous work (revised 9 times before publication, 5 times thereafter and again for the French edition, 1790) has still to be made. For the many printed observations and strictures on Burke's *Reflections* see *Cambridge Bibliography of English Literature* II, pp. 634–5.

SPEECH ON THE ARMY ESTIMATES (1790).

A LETTER TO A MEMBER OF THE NATIONAL ASSEMBLY (1791).

AN APPEAL FROM THE NEW TO THE OLD WHIGS (1791).

A LETTER TO SIR HERCULES LANGRISHE ON THE SUBJECT OF THE ROMAN CATHOLICS OF IRELAND (1792).

SUBSTANCE OF THE SPEECH . . . IN ANSWER TO CERTAIN OBSERVATIONS IN THE REPORT OF THE COMMITTEE OF MANAGERS [OF THE IMPEACHMENT OF WARREN HASTINGS] (1794).

THOUGHTS AND DETAILS ON SCARCITY [1795].

A LETTER TO A NOBLE LORD ON THE ATTACKS MADE UPON HIM AND HIS PENSION IN THE HOUSE OF LORDS (1796).
Burke continued to revise the text through the first 10 of the 13 editions or issues of 1796—a striking example of the textual difficulties, still unresolved, facing an editor.

TWO LETTERS . . . ON THE PROPOSALS FOR PEACE, WITH THE REGICIDE DIRECTORY OF FRANCE (1796).
A third letter appeared in 1797 and a fourth (written 1795) in Vol. 5 of *Works*, 1812.

TWO LETTERS ON THE CONDUCT OF OUR DOMESTIC PARTIES (1797).

Some Biographical and Critical Studies:

MEMOIRS OF BURKE, by C. McCormick (1797).

THE LIFE, by R. Bisset. 2 vols. (1800).

MEMOIR OF THE LIFE AND CHARACTER, by Sir J. Prior (1824).

A MEMOIR OF THE POLITICAL LIFE, by G. Croly. 2 vols. (1840).

THE CHARACTER OF EDMUND BURKE, by F. H. Clack (1845).

THE PUBLIC AND DOMESTIC LIFE, by P. Burke (1854).

THE CHARACTER OF EDMUND BURKE, by H. M. Butler (1854).

HISTORY OF THE LIFE AND TIMES, by T. Macknight. 3 vols. (1858–60).

BURKE, by J. Morley (1879).
In the English Men of Letters Series.

EDMUND BURKE: A STUDY OF HIS LIFE AND CHARACTER, by E. A. Parkhurst (1886).

EDMUND BURKE, APOSTLE OF JUSTICE AND LIBERTY, by T. S. Pillans (1905).

THE POLITICAL LIFE, by N. Spinelli (1908).

THE POLITICAL PHILOSOPHY, by J. McCunn (1913).

THE EARLY LIFE, CORRESPONDENCE AND WRITINGS, by A. P. I. Samuels. Cambridge (1923).
Some of Burke's early writings are printed here for the first time.

EDMUND BURKE AS AN IRISHMAN, by W. O'Brien (1924).

EDMUND BURKE, by B. Newman (1927).

EDMUND BURKE AND THE REVOLT AGAINST THE EIGHTEENTH CENTURY, by A. Cobban (1929).

BURKE AND BRISTOL, 1774–1780, by E. Barker. Bristol (1931).

BURKE, by P. Magnus (1939).

BURKE AND ROUSSEAU, by A. M. Osborn (1940).

BURKE, by G. M. Young (1943).
The Annual Lecture on a Master Mind, to the British Academy.

EDMUND BURKE, by H. Laski (1947).
An Address on the occasion of the bi-centenary of the foundation of Burke's 'Club'.

EDMUND BURKE, CHRISTIAN STATESMAN, by E. E. Reynolds (1948).

EDMUND BURKE, SIX ESSAYS, by T. W. Copeland (1950).

OUR LEGACY FROM BURKE, by L. Barry (1952).

THE MORAL BASIS OF BURKE'S POLITICAL THOUGHT, by C. Parkin (1956).

WRITERS AND THEIR WORK

Available at 2s. net each; starred titles 1s. 6d. net each

MATTHEW ARNOLD: Kenneth Allott
JANE AUSTEN*: Sylvia Townsend
  Warner
HILAIRE BELLOC: Renée Haynes
ARNOLD BENNETT*: Frank
  Swinnerton
WILLIAM BLAKE*: Kathleen Raine
JAMES BOSWELL: P. A. W. Collins
ELIZABETH BOWEN: Jocelyn Brooke
THE BRONTË SISTERS: P. Bentley
BUNYAN: Henri Talon
SAMUEL BUTLER: G. D. H. Cole
BYRON*: Herbert Read
THOMAS CARLYLE*: David
  Gascoyne
JOYCE CARY: Walter Allen
CHAUCER: Nevill Coghill
G. K. CHESTERTON: Christopher Hollis
WINSTON CHURCHILL: John Connell
COLERIDGE: Kathleen Raine
R. G. COLLINGWOOD: E. W. F.
  Tomlin
I. COMPTON-BURNETT*: Pamela
  Hansford Johnson
JOSEPH CONRAD: Oliver Warner
GEORGE CRABBE: R. L. Brett
C. DAY LEWIS: Clifford Dyment
DEFOE: J. R. Sutherland
CHARLES DICKENS: K. J. Fielding
DONNE: Frank Kermode
NORMAN DOUGLAS: Ian Greenlees
JOHN DRYDEN: Bonamy Dobrée
GEORGE ELIOT*: Lettice Cooper
T. S. ELIOT: M. C. Bradbrook
FIELDING: John Butt
FORD MADOX FORD: Kenneth Young
E. M. FORSTER: Rex Warner
CHRISTOPHER FRY: Derek Stanford
EDWARD GIBBON: C. V. Wedgwood
ROBERT GRAVES: M. Seymour-Smith
GRAHAM GREENE: Francis Wyndham ·
JOHN GALSWORTHY: R. H. Mottram
THOMAS HARDY*: R. A. Scott-James
G. M. HOPKINS: Geoffrey Grigson
A. E. HOUSMAN: Ian Scott-Kilvert
ALDOUS HUXLEY: Jocelyn Brooke
HENRY JAMES: Michael Swan
SAMUEL JOHNSON: S. C. Roberts
JOHN KEATS: Edmund Blunden

RUDYARD KIPLING*: Bonamy Dobrée
CHARLES LAMB: Edmund Blunden
D. H. LAWRENCE: Kenneth Young
WYNDHAM LEWIS: E. W. F. Tomlin
KATHERINE MANSFIELD: Ian A.
  Gordon
WALTER DE LA MARE: Kenneth
  Hopkins
CHRISTOPHER MARLOWE: Philip
  Henderson
JOHN MASEFIELD*: L. A. G. Strong
SOMERSET MAUGHAM*: John
  Brophy
MILTON: E. M. W. Tillyard
WILLIAM MORRIS: Philip Henderson
EDWIN MUIR: J. C. Hall
JOHN HENRY NEWMAN:
  J. M. Cameron
GEORGE ORWELL: Tom Hopkinson
POPE: Ian Jack
J. B. PRIESTLEY: Ivor Brown
HERBERT READ: Francis Berry
D. G. ROSSETTI: Oswald Doughty
RUSKIN: Peter Quennell
BERTRAND RUSSELL*: Alan Dorward
BERNARD SHAW*: A. C. Ward
SHAKESPEARE: C. J. Sisson
SHELLEY: Stephen Spender
SHERIDAN*: W. A. Darlington
EDITH SITWELL: John Lehmann
OSBERT SITWELL*: Roger Fulford
TOBIAS SMOLLETT*: Laurence
  Brander
STERNE: D. W. Jefferson
R. L. STEVENSON: G. B. Stern
LYTTON STRACHEY: R. A.
  Scott-James
SWIFT: J. Middleton Murry
SWINBURNE: H. J. C. Grierson
TENNYSON: F. L. Lucas
G. M. TREVELYAN*: J. H. Plumb
EVELYN WAUGH: Christopher Hollis
H. G. WELLS: Montgomery Belgion
OSCAR WILDE: James Laver
CHARLES WILLIAMS: J. Heath-Stubbs
IZAAK WALTON: Margaret Bottrall
VIRGINIA WOOLF: Bernard Blackstone
WORDSWORTH: Helen Darbishire
W. B. YEATS: G. S. Fraser

*The first 55 issues in the Series appeared under the
General Editorship of* T. O. BEACHCROFT

¶ Essays in active preparation include assessments of Spenser, Horace Walpole, Burns, W. H. Auden, Dylan Thomas and other classics and contemporaries.

WRITERS AND THEIR WORK

★

A NEW ISSUE in this series on Writers and their Work is published monthly and may be ordered from any bookseller or, in case of difficulty, direct from the Publishers, LONGMANS, GREEN & CO. LTD., 6 & 7 Clifford Street, London W.1.

Annual subscription (12 issues)   22s. 6d. post free
Six months' subscription (6 issues)   12s. post free
Single issues   2s. each
(Back numbers available at 1s. 6d. and 2s. each—for list of titles see inside cover.)

★

BRITISH BOOK NEWS, to which these essays form supplements, is published monthly and may be obtained from The British Council, 59 New Oxford Street, London W.C.1. In addition to an article of general or bibliographical interest, each issue contains short, informative and critical reviews, by specialists, of some 200 books. Every subject is covered, including fiction and children's books, and full details of publisher, price, size, etc., are given. Annual subscription: U.K. 30s.★; U.S.A. and Canada $4.25★; other countries 15s.★

★With Annual Index